Music & Movement

IN THE
Classroom

Grades 1–2

WRITTEN BY Steven Traugh

Featuring the songs of Youngheart Music's
Greg Scelsa and Steve Millang

EDITOR	Cindy Truitt
ILLUSTRATOR	Catherine Rader
COVER PHOTOGRAPHER	Michael Jarrett
DESIGNER	Moonhee Pak
COVER DESIGNER	Moonhee Pak
ART DIRECTOR	Tom Cochrane
PROJECT DIRECTOR	Carolea Williams

© 2000 Creative Teaching Press, Inc., Huntington Beach, CA 92649
© 1993 Creative Teaching Press, Inc., Cypress, CA 90630
© 1989 Kiducation, Revised Edition 1993

Table of Contents

Introduction

Music & Movement in the Classroom is a complete program of materials and teaching techniques designed to channel children's natural enthusiasm for music and movement into productive learning experiences. Designed for the elementary teacher, this program features clear step-by-step lesson plans along with exciting and engaging songs and stories that make teaching enjoyable for the musical novice and expert alike.

The program outlined in this book is easy to integrate into your weekly lesson plans. The 30-lesson developmental curriculum provides one 20–25 minute lesson per week. Each lesson introduces a new song and movement activity, to be followed by a 20–25 minute review that same week.

Each lesson reinforces the skill and content taught in reading, writing, social studies, and science. Counting, sequencing, and pattern recognition become meaningful to children in lessons that use the relationship between rhythm and math. Singing activities use the lyrics of songs to enhance vocabulary, oral expression, and reading.

Use this program to meet the needs of each child. By offering a wide variety of experiences that include listening and moving, these lessons allow you to teach to the children's strongest learning modalities. Lessons have a profound impact, which results in a longer attention span and greater retention.

The activities in *Music & Movement in the Classroom* encourage self-expression. The performance activities offer opportunities for children to use their own creativity and to work with others. They see their own potential and growth in self-esteem, as well as in their appreciation of each other.

How to Use These Materials

This curriculum lends itself to many classroom applications. The presentation and structure of the materials in this book and on the CDs have been designed for the teacher who finds music and movement to be new or unfamiliar areas of the curriculum. The 30 lessons are presented in a developmental progression that has been proven effective in a wide variety of first- and second-grade settings. However, for the teacher who already uses music and movement in the classroom, the order and content of the materials can be altered and adapted to supplement the existing program.

Each activity page includes objectives and skills reinforced in the lesson. In preparation for most lessons, you may want to make a transparency of the lyric page to display on an overhead projecter for children to see. Give a copy of each lyric page to children to color and keep in a folder. Or, enlarge a copy of each lyric page, decorate it, and display it on a bulletin board.

This curriculum is designed for the needs and abilities of a wide variety of first- and second-grade students. You are encouraged to adapt these materials to meet the needs of your class. Students need not have received Music & Movement in the Classroom instruction at previous grade levels in order to be successful with the activities presented in any successive grade level.

The Lessons

1. Schedule 20 to 25 minutes of instruction at a regular time twice a week (a total of 40 to 50 minutes of weekly instruction). Introduce each lesson on the first day of weekly music instruction, and reinforce it on a second day that same week.

2. The lessons generally fall into one of three categories:
   • movement activities
   • singing activities
   • rhythmic activities
   Lessons in all three areas progress from easy introductory activities to more challenging applications. Successive lessons vary in the type of activity.

3. Each lesson should be done with a review of the previous lesson's activity. This is done for two reasons:
   • Students increase their level of performance with the additional participation that a review provides.
   • The main activity of the lesson combined with the review activity allows students to participate in a variety of activities each week.

4. Begin each lesson with a vocal warm-up. Have the class warm up their voices by making a sliding sound that moves from a low pitch to a high pitch and back to a low pitch again—like a siren. Do this several times, reminding children not to yell.

Scheduling

The typical school year contains 36 to 38 weeks of instruction. At the rate of one lesson per week, this curriculum requires 30 weeks to complete. The lessons in this curriculum are divided into two sections. Each section contains fifteen lessons. Teachers with traditional schedules should plan to complete Lessons 1 through 15 the first semester and Lessons 16 through 30 the second semester. Teachers on year-round tracks should plan to complete approximately eight lessons for each of the nine-week sessions. (Other year-round configurations will require adjustments to this schedule.)

The Compact Discs

Two CDs are included with the book for this curriculum. The CDs contain all the music used in the lessons. Each activity page lists the music and track number(s) for that lesson.

1

The Freeze

Objective

♪ To develop creativity with steady beat movements to music

Skills

♪ Movement

♪ Rhythm

♪ Listening

♪ Creativity

♪ Leadership

Music

CD #1, Track 1: "The Freeze"

ACTIVITY

1 Have children stand facing you. Make sure they have enough space to move their bodies freely.

2 Tell children that the song "The Freeze" has six sections. At the end of each section, the music stops, "freezing" the beat.

3 Play "The Freeze." Use the directions in the song to lead children in a different movement for each section of the music.

4 Repeat the same movement until you hear the music stop, and then have children "freeze" in position. When the music resumes, proceed with a new steady beat movement.

EXTENSION

Choose six children who would like to be movement leaders. Have each child lead a movement during one of the six sections of the music. Ask each leader to create a different movement. Encourage children to be creative. Arrange the leaders in the correct sequence according to the part they lead in the music. Play "The Freeze," and have the class follow the movements of each leader. Choose six new leaders to repeat the activity.

The Freeze

Words and Music by Greg Scelsa Copyright
1978, Little House Music and Gregorian
Chance Music (ASCAP)

Now here's a game that's kinda neat.
Just get your body in the beat.
But when you hear the music quit,
Don't want to see you move a bit.
Now you can dance any way you please,
But listen closely for the freeze.

Instrumental Interlude

Now you can hop and you can bop,
And you can flip and you can flop,
And you can rock and roll with style and ease,
And you can bump and you can hustle,
But don't ever move a muscle,
When you hear the music come in to the freeze.

Say Hello

Objectives

♪ To practice echo singing

♪ To use singing as a means of greeting new people and making friends

Skills

♪ Singing

♪ Listening

♪ Reading

Music

CD #1, Track 2: "Say Hello"

ACTIVITY

1 In advance, write the lyrics of the song "Say Hello" on chart paper or an overhead transparency. Display the lyrics for the class to see.

2 Some children tend to yell instead of sing, especially when they get excited. Tell children to smile while they sing. It's almost impossible to smile and yell at the same time.

3 Play "Say Hello." Have the class echo sing the song with the children's voices in the music.

4 Track the song lyrics as the class sings.

EXTENSIONS

• Once children become familiar with "Say Hello," divide the class into two groups. Have the first group sing the lead part with the music. Have the second group echo in response. Have groups switch roles and repeat the activity.

• Help children create movements that dramatize each line in the song. Have them practice the movements as you read the corresponding line of the lyrics. Play "Say Hello." As children sing, lead them in performing the movements they created.

• Discuss the importance of friendship. Ask children to suggest ways to make a new classmate feel comfortable in the class, and record their ideas. Assign one idea from the list to each child, and have children illustrate their idea. Bind the pages into a class book, or use them for a classroom bulletin board.

Say Hello

Words and Music by Christopher Moroney
Copyright 1985, Little House Music and Gregorian
Chance Music (ASCAP)

Say "Hello."
I would like to get to know you.
Let's be friends.
Say "Hello."
Look at all the friendly faces
In the world.

Oh, we all
Live together
In a world
That we share.

So shake hands
With your neighbors.
Let them know
That you're there.

Say "Hello."
Let a smile come shinin' through you.
Let it shine.
Say "Hello."

(Getting softer)
Say "Hello."

(Whisper)
Say "Hello."

(Loud)
Say "Hello."

Say "Hello."
I would like to get to know you.
Let's be friends.
Say "Hello."
Look at all the friendly faces
In the world.

Oh, we all
Live together
In a world
That we share.

So shake hands
With your neighbors.
Let them know
That you're there.

Say "Hello."
Let a smile come shinin' through you.
Let it shine.
Say "Hello."

(Getting softer)
Say "Hello."

(Whisper)
Say "Hello."

(Loud)
Say "Hello."

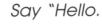

3

Count and Move

Objectives

♪ To improve counting skills

♪ To listen to directions and execute tasks

♪ To improve coordination

ACTIVITY

1 Have children stand an arm's length apart and face you.

2 Ask them to listen carefully to the music you are about to play and follow you as you do the movements described in the song.

3 Play the song "Count and Move." Have the class perform the movements as you model them to the beat of the music. Repeat as desired.

EXTENSIONS

• Have children make up new movements to "Count and Move." List the movements on chart paper. Select children who wish to lead the class in performing the new movements with the music.

• Use this activity when teaching children to count by twos, fives, and/or tens.

Skills

♪ Listening

♪ Counting

♪ Movement

♪ Coordination

Music

CD #1, Track 3: "Count and Move"

Count and Move

Words and Music by Steven Traugh
Copyright 1991, Kiducation (ASCAP)

Let's begin by clapping our hands and counting to 10. Ready, go!
1-2-3-4-5-6-7-8-9-10

Do it again.
1-2-3-4-5-6-7-8-9-10

Ready, now pat your legs and count to 13. Go!
1-2-3-4-5-6-7-8-9-10-11-12-13

Tap your shoulders and count to 8. Go!
1-2-3-4-5-6-7-8

Pat your stomach and count to 17. Go!
1-2-3-4-5-6-7-8-9-10-11-12-13-14-15-16-17

Hop on one foot and count to 12. Go!
1-2-3-4-5-6-7-8-9-10-11-12

Tap your nose and count to 19. Go!
1-2-3-4-5-6-7-8-9-10-11-12-13-14-15-16-17-18-19

Now touch your toes and count to 7. Go!
1-2-3-4-5-6-7

Now tap your cheeks and count to 14. Go!
1-2-3-4-5-6-7-8-9-10-11-12-13-14

Okay, now do the twist and count to 9. Go!
1-2-3-4-5-6-7-8-9

Tap your fingertips and count to 16. Go!
1-2-3-4-5-6-7-8-9-10-11-12-13-14-15-16

Stamp your foot and count to 11. Go!
1-2-3-4-5-6-7-8-9-10-11

Now pat your head and count to 6. Go!
1-2-3-4-5-6

Ready, now tap your knees and count to 15. Go!
1-2-3-4-5-6-7-8-9-10-11-12-13-14-15

Now tap your eyebrows and count to 18. Go!
1-2-3-4-5-6-7-8-9-10-11-12-13-14-15-16-17-18

Okay, now pull your ears and count to 5. Go!
1-2-3-4-5

Everybody jump and count to 20. Go!
1-2-3-4-5-6-7-8-9-10-11-12-13-14-15-16-17-18-19-20

Piggy Bank

Objectives

♪ To learn the number of cents in a nickel, dime, quarter, half-dollar, and dollar

♪ To improve singing skills

Skills

♪ Listening

♪ Singing

♪ Spelling

Music

CD #1, Track 4: "Piggy Bank"

ACTIVITY

1. In advance, photocopy a class set of the Piggy Bank Spelling Game reproducible (page 62).

2. Give each child a sheet. Tell the class that the Piggy Bank Spelling Game contains most of the words to the song "Piggy Bank." Tell them to carefully listen to the song.

3. Play "Piggy Bank." Help the class fill in the letters of the missing words by modeling on a chalkboard or an overhead transparency. Pause the song if necessary.

4. Play the song a second time. Have children track the lyrics from their sheet.

EXTENSIONS

- Have children read aloud the lyrics from their completed sheet.

- Read the first half of each line to the class. Have children respond by reading the second half of each line. Switch roles and repeat the activity.

Piggy Bank

Words and Music by Greg Scelsa
Copyright 1979, Little House Music and Gregorian
Chance Music (ASCAP)

One penny is just a cent.
Five pennies make a nickel.
Ten pennies make a dime.
Twenty-five pennies make a quarter.
Fifty pennies make a half-dollar.
One hundred pennies make a dollar.
One dollar is what I'm saving in my piggy bank.

Aerobics A–Z

Objectives

♪ To improve phonemic awareness skills

♪ To listen to directions and execute tasks

♪ To improve coordination

Skills

♪ Listening

♪ Phonemic Awareness

♪ Movement

♪ Coordination

♪ Group Cooperation

Music

CD #1, Track 5: "Aerobics A–Z"

ACTIVITY

1. In advance, use a premade chart or letter cards to create an alphabet display.

2. Have children face you and stand at least an arm's length apart in all directions.

3. Tell the class that they are about to hear some music that will help them distinguish the sound of each letter in the alphabet.

4. Play the song "Aerobics A–Z." Point to each letter on the display. Have the class move with you as you model the movements to the beat of the music. Repeat as desired.

EXTENSIONS

- Have volunteers lead the class in performing the movements with the song.

- Display the lyrics to "Aerobics A–Z." Have children find the words that include the sound of the letter featured in each verse.

- Have each child select a different verse of the lyric to illustrate. Combine the pages into a class songbook.

Aerobics A-Z

Words and Music by Steven Traugh
Copyright 1991, Kiducation (ASCAP)

A – arms in the air, circling 'round and around
B – bounce your body like a basketball
C – curl into a crouch and creep like a cat
D – dig a deep ditch down in the dirt
E – elevate your elbows and count to eleven
F – flex your fingers and fan your face
G – get on your giraffe and gallop on the grass
H – hands on hips and hop on one foot
I – imitate an inchworm inching along
J – join into the jam with jumping jacks
K – kiss a kitten while you knock your knees
L – lift each leg lightly toward the lights
M – move your mouth as you munch your lunch
N – nod with your neck and nudge with your nose
O – outswim an otter in the ocean—go
P – push and pull with the palms of your hands
Q – quiver quickly like a shivering, quivering quail
R – run a race with a raccoon and a rabbit
S – skip, skip, skip and try not to slip
T – tap your tummy, then tap your toes
U – coil and uncoil like an undulating snake
V – vacuum the room with a voom, voom, voom
W – wiggle your waist and wiggle your wrists
X – exercise like a Tyrannosaurus rex
Y – yawn with a yearning for a year-long nap
Z – fall asleep and catch some Zs

6

B-A Bay

Objectives

♪ To recognize long vowel sounds

♪ To improve singing skills

Skills

♪ Singing

♪ Concentration

Music

CD #1, Tracks 6 and 7: "B–A Bay #1" and "B–A Bay #2"

ACTIVITY

1 In advance, display the lyrics of the song "B–A Bay" on chart paper or an overhead transparency.

2 Tell the class that they are going to learn a singing game and hear long vowel sounds.

3 Read each line of the first verse, and have children echo in response.

4 Play "B–A Bay #1." Have children sing along with the music as you track the words.

5 Have volunteers track the lyrics while the rest of the class reads and sings along.

EXTENSIONS

• Have children create a new version of the song by replacing the beginning consonant in each verse.

• Have children illustrate the new verses to the song, and use their work for a class book or bulletin board display.

• Invite the class to sing and dramatize the new verses with "B–A Bay #2" (an instrumental version of the song).

B-A Bay

Words and Music by Steven Traugh
Copyright 1992, Kiducation (ASCAP)

B-A bay,
B-E bee,
B-I bidey bi,
B-O bo,
Bidey bi bo,
B-U bu,
Bidey bi bo bu, bu.

Come on now and sing along.
It's not hard to do.
Just pick a consonant and sing,
With an A-E-I-O-U.

K-A kay,
K-E key,
K-I kidey ki,
K-O ko,
Kidey ki ko,
K-U ku,
Kidey ki ko ku, ku.

M-A may,
M-E me,
M-I midey mi,
M-O mo,
Midey mi mo,
M-U mu,
Midey mi mo mu, mu.

Come on now and sing along.
It's not hard to do.
Just pick a consonant and sing,
With an A-E-I-O-U.

Z-A zay,
Z-E zee,
Z-I zidey zi,
Z-O zo,
Zidey zi zo,
Z-U zu,
Zidey zi zo zu, zu.
Z-A, Z-E, Z-I, Z-O, Z-U
Zu, zu, zu!

LESSON

7

Nocturne

Objectives

♪ To move in slow motion

♪ To create movements that tell a story or describe an action

♪ To improve coordination

Skills

♪ Concentration

♪ Movement

Music

CD #1, Track 8: "Nocturne"

ACTIVITY

1 Have the class stand where they have room to move their arms and legs.

2 Tell children that they are about to practice moving in slow motion.

3 Play the instrumental "Nocturne," and lead the class in slow motion movements. To develop their slow motion movement skills, concentrate on different parts of the body. Use the following movements as a guide:
- move fingers (on one hand and then on both hands)
- move arms (one and then both)
- move head (including facial expressions)
- move upper torso
- move legs and feet (one and then both)
- move a combination of body parts

EXTENSION

Select a volunteer to demonstrate movements in slow motion that depict familiar activities. For example, a child can pantomime
- unlocking and opening a door
- making a sandwich and taking a bite
- casting a line and catching a fish
- looking up a number and making a telephone call

Write the list of activities on chart paper. Have the whole class practice the new movements to "Nocturne."

Nocturne
Music by Greg Scelsa
Copyright 1978, Little House Music and Gregorian Chance Music (ASCAP)

Months of the Year

Objective

♪ To learn the months of the year

ACTIVITY

1 In advance, write the months of the year on a chalkboard or an overhead transparency.

2 Play the song "Months of the Year #1." Point to each month as it is mentioned in the song.

3 Erase the first letter of each month. Have the class listen to the song, and tell them to be ready to fill in the blank spaces with letters that complete the name of each month.

4 Play "Months of the Year #1" again. Have volunteers fill in the blank spaces with the correct letters.

5 Then, have children practice reading the entire list as you point to the months in a random order.

6 Have children practice singing with the music.

Skills

♪ Listening

♪ Spelling

♪ Singing

EXTENSION

Teach the class the months of the year in Spanish: enero, febrero, marzo, abril, mayo, junio, julio, agosto, septiembre, octubre, noviembre, and diciembre. Play "Months of the Year #2," the Spanish version of the song. Have the class sing along.

Music

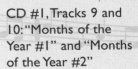

CD #1, Tracks 9 and 10: "Months of the Year #1" and "Months of the Year #2"

Months of the Year

Words and Music by Greg Scelsa
Copyright 1978, Little House Music and
Gregorian Chance Music (ASCAP)

January,
February,
March and April,
May and June and July,
August,
September,
October,
November, December.

(Repeat)

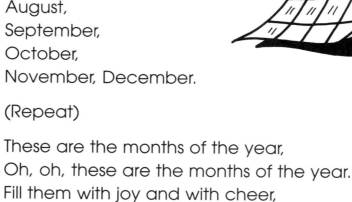

These are the months of the year,
Oh, oh, these are the months of the year.
Fill them with joy and with cheer,
The months of the year.

Enero,
Febrero,
Marzo,
Abril,
Mayo y junio y julio,
Agosto,
Septiembre,
Octubre,
Noviembre,
Diciembre.

(Repeat)

These are the months of the year,
Oh, oh, these are the months of the year.
Fill them with joy and with cheer,
The months of the year.

Just Like Me

ACTIVITY

1 Have children stand in an area where they can move their arms freely. Divide the class into pairs. Have one person in each pair create simple movements in slow motion for the other to mirror. Offer the following movements as a guide:
- move fingers (on one hand and then on both hands)
- move arms (one and then both)
- move head (including facial expressions)
- move upper torso
- move legs and feet (one and then both)
- move a combination of body parts

2 Play the song "Just Like Me." Have leaders demonstrate the movements to the music while their partners follow.

3 Have partners switch roles and repeat the activity. This will give each child a turn to lead and follow. Have children switch roles approximately every 30 seconds.

4 As children become skilled, allow them to create movements that become gradually faster. Tell them to repeat fast movements over and over so their partner has time to learn to imitate the movements.

EXTENSION

Once children are skilled at following their partners, divide the class into groups of three or four. Have one child be the leader and create new slow motion movements for the rest of the group to follow. Have children practice with the music. Repeat this activity, allowing each child a turn to be the group leader.

Objective

♪ To create and follow movements

Skills

♪ Movement

♪ Concentration

Music

CD #1, Track 11: "Just Like Me"

Just Like Me

Words and Music by Greg Scelsa Copyright 1980,
Little House Music and Gregorian Chance Music
(ASCAP)

This is a funny game
That's very, very easy to play.
Whatever way I move,
You do it in the very same way.
Pretend you're looking in a mirror.
Do everything that you see.
Now do it just like me!

Instrumental Interlude

Well if I blink my eyes,
You blink yours, too.
If I shake my thighs,
Well you shake yours, too.
If I move around in a real slow motion,
Do what you see.
Now do it just like me.

(Repeat)

Let's Go to the Market

ACTIVITY

1 In advance, write the lyrics of the song "Let's Go to the Market" on chart paper or an overhead transparency. Display the lyrics for the class to see.

2 Read the lyrics one line at a time. Have children echo in response.

3 Have each child illustrate one of the foods listed in the song. Play "Let's Go to the Market" while children draw.

4 Then, tell the class that they are going to play a game about foods found in a market. Explain that as the voice in the song sings about buying a certain food, they should pantomime picking up that food and putting it into their shopping cart. Remind them to follow the beat of the music as they move.

5 Have children stand and create a line that will snake in and around their desks to form the aisles of the supermarket. Sort their pictures into food groups (as mentioned in the song), and place them along the aisles. Demonstrate which direction they will go around the room in search of healthy food.

6 Play "Let's Go to the Market." Have children "shop" as they dramatize the lyrics of the song. Repeat as desired.

EXTENSIONS

- Write the six food groups (i.e., vegetables; fruits; bread, cereal, and pasta; meat, poultry, and fish; milk, yogurt, and cheese; and fats, oils, and sweets) in columns on the chalkboard. Ask children to name foods they know for each group. List their answers in the correct columns.

- Have children bring in vegetables to make vegetable soup. Read aloud *Stone Soup* by Marcia Brown (Scribner) while children eat their soup.

Objectives

♪ To improve singing skills

♪ To dramatize the lyrics of a song

♪ To learn to categorize food groups

Skills

♪ Singing

♪ Dramatic Movement

♪ Listening

Music

CD #1, Track 12: "Let's Go to the Market"

Let's Go to the Market

Words and Music by Frank Leto and Greg Scelsa
Copyright 1994, Little House Music (ASCAP)

Chorus:
    Come on, let's go,
    Come on, let's go,
    Come on, let's go to the market.
    We're gonna buy some healthy food.

We're gonna buy some vegetables.
Fill the basket up with . . .
Lettuce,
Celery,
Broccoli,
Zucchini,
Tomatoes,
Potatoes,
Carrots,
And corn.

(Chorus)

We're gonna buy some grains.
Fill the basket up with . . .
Wheat bread,
Bagels,
Crackers,
Tortillas,
Pasta,
Granola,
Oatmeal,
And rice.

(Chorus)

We're gonna buy some fruit.
Fill the basket up with . . .
Apples,
Strawberries,
Grapefruit,
Bananas,
Peaches,
Nectarines,
Watermelon
And grapes.

(Chorus)

We're gonna buy some protein.
Fill the basket up with . . .
Chicken,
Soybeans,
Hamburger,
Cottage cheese,
Yogurt,
Fresh fish,
Peanut butter,
And eggs.

(Chorus)

We're gonna buy what's good to eat.
Yeah!

Disco Limbo

ACTIVITY

1 Have children stand and count to four as they walk in place, then rest four counts, and then repeat.

2 Have children clap their hands once for each step they take. Encourage them to concentrate on counting, clapping, and stepping at the same time.

3 Increase the number of steps and rests to eight.

4 Play a portion of the song "Disco Limbo." Have children practice walking in place to the beat of the music.

5 Substitute steady beat hand movements for the eight-count rests between each group of eight steps. Have children practice these steady beat movements with the music:
- snap fingers
- tap elbows
- tap fingertips
- flap "wings"
- knock knees

6 Have two children hold up a "limbo stick" (e.g., yardstick, broom handle, pointer, or any available prop that is safe and convenient).

7 Have children form a single line in front of the limbo stick. Play "Disco Limbo." Have children take turns bending backward and walking under the limbo stick in time with the beat of the music.

8 Lead the class in eight counts of walking and eight counts of steady beat movements as they wait their turn to go under the limbo stick.

EXTENSION

Have children pretend to drive vehicles under a bridge. Encourage them to be creative. Suggest they drive a car, ride a bicycle, or fly under the bridge. Allow children to go under the bridge one at a time as they pretend to drive a vehicle. Have the rest of the class guess what the vehicle is.

Objectives

♪ To create steady beat movements with legs and feet

♪ To perform a line dance called "the limbo"

Skills

♪ Rhythm

♪ Coordination

♪ Group Cooperation

Music

CD #1, Track 13: "Disco Limbo"

Disco Limbo

Words and Music by Greg Scelsa
Copyright 1979, Little House Music and Gregorian
Chance Music (ASCAP)

All right, everybody disco limbo.
Oh, oh, let's do the disco limbo.
Everybody take a turn an' do the disco limbo.
Oh, oh, let's do the disco limbo.
Come on and take a turn.
Do the disco limbo.
You can do it,
Yes, ya can,
Yes, ya can.
Everybody do the limbo.

Instrumental Interlude

There's a dance they do in Jamaica
That will make ya want to laugh.
Get yourself a limbo bar and see how low you go.
Bend your legs and lean way back.
Now you've got the trick.
Slip your body underneath the disco limbo stick. Hey!

(Repeat)

Music & Movement in the Classroom Grades 1–2 © 2000 Creative Teaching Press

Purple Cow

ACTIVITY

1 In advance, write the lyrics of the song "Purple Cow" on sentence strips. (Note that only the first line of each verse changes and the rest of the text remains the same.) Display the strips in a pocket chart.

2 Read aloud one line at a time, and have children echo in response.

3 Play "Purple Cow." Have the class read and sing along. Repeat as desired. At the end of the song, ask
- *What was unusual about the animals in this song?*
- *Could these animals be real? Why or why not?*
- *Do you think the animals were real or fantasy?*

EXTENSIONS

- Have children illustrate the animals in "Purple Cow." Play the song while they draw.

- Have children use paper bags and crayons to make silly animal masks. Have them create a "Purple Cow Parade" by marching around the room to the beat of the song.

- Have children work in small groups to rewrite the lyrics of the song using their own fantasy creatures.

- Use this lesson as a springboard to a larger study on the relationship of animal coloration and habitat.

Objectives

♪ To learn the song "Purple Cow"

♪ To learn the concepts of fantasy and reality

♪ To create fantasy creatures

Skills

♪ Singing

♪ Listening

♪ Reading

♪ Writing

♪ Creativity

Music

CD #1, Track 14: "Purple Cow"

Purple Cow

Words and Music by Steven Traugh Copyright
1995, Kiducation (ASCAP)

I've never seen a purple cow.
I'd really like to see one.
But I can tell you anyhow,
I'd rather see than be one.

Chorus:
  Let's all make a silly zoo,
  And mix up all the colors,
  With purple cows and pink baboons.
  Can you think of any others?

I've never seen a green giraffe.
I'd really like to see one.
But I can tell you anyhow,
I'd rather see than be one.

(Chorus)

I've never seen a red elephant.
I'd really like to see one.
But I can tell you anyhow,
I'd rather see than be one.

(Chorus)

I've never seen a yellow hippo.
I'd really like to see one.
But I can tell you anyhow,
I'd rather see than be one.

(Chorus)

I've never seen an orange ostrich.
I'd really like to see one.
But I can tell you anyhow,
I'd rather see than be one.

(Chorus)

I've never seen a blue porcupine.
I'd really like to see one.
But I can tell you anyhow,
I'd rather see than be one.

(Chorus)

Reading Rhythmic Notation #1

ACTIVITY

1 In advance, draw Example 1 on chart paper or the chalkboard.

Example 1

clap clap clap clap   rest rest rest rest

2 Tell the class that the symbols in the first measure are one type of steady beat called *notes*. Tell them to clap on each note.

3 Have children practice counting to four while reading and clapping the first measure of Example 1. Point to each note as children count and clap together.

4 Point to the symbols in the second measure. Explain that they are another type of steady beat called *rests*. Tell them not to clap on a rest. Have children practice reading (clapping and resting) both measures. Point to each note or rest as you count slowly to four.

5 Draw Example 2 on the board.

Example 2

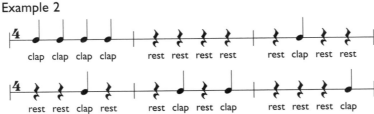

clap clap clap clap   rest rest rest rest   rest clap rest rest

rest rest clap rest   rest clap rest clap   rest rest rest clap

6 Have the class practice reading (clapping and resting) the notation of Example 2. Point to each note or rest as you count slowly to four throughout each measure with the class.

EXTENSION

Have half the class use rhythm instruments to perform the examples while the rest of the class claps the beat. Have children switch roles so that everyone gets a turn to clap and play an instrument.

Objectives

♪ To read quarter notes and rests as units of a steady beat

♪ To perform rhythmic notation as a group

Skills

♪ Reading

♪ Rhythm

♪ Concentration

Music

There is no music for this lesson.

14

Hand Jive

Objectives

♪ To clap accents and rhythm patterns

♪ To recite poetry with rhythmic precision

Skills

♪ Listening

♪ Reading

♪ Voice Expression

♪ Rhythm

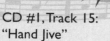

Music

CD #1, Track 15: "Hand Jive"

ACTIVITY

1 In advance, make copies of the lyrics to the song "Hand Jive." Give a copy to each child.

2 Play "Hand Jive." Have children clap the accents and rhythm patterns as directed by the voice in the recording.

3 Read aloud the song line by line. Have children echo in response while they read from their sheet.

4 Have the class practice reciting the phrases with the music. Have children work on imitating the rhythm and inflection of the voice in the recording.

EXTENSION

Have three volunteers lead the movements in "Hand Jive." Ask each volunteer to recite one verse and lead the class in clapping the rhythm that follows the music. Select new volunteers to lead the class. Repeat as desired.

Hand Jive

Words and Music by Greg Scelsa Copyright
1980, Little House Music
and Gregorian Chance Music (ASCAP)

Here's a rhythm game with a crazy name
They call the Hand Jive.
All you do is put five fingers
Together with the other five,
And you clap like this . . .

(Clap on second beat. Repeat eight times.)

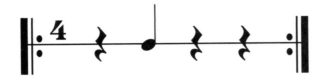

Now I know you've got this rhythm down,
Gonna jive just a little bit more.
This time put your hands together
On the rhythm of two and four,
And clap like this . . .

(Clap on second and fourth beats. Repeat eight times.)

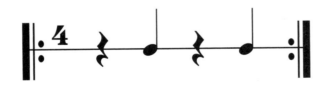

Now let's take this rhythm all the way,
'Cause you know it's kinda neat.
Everybody do the Hand Jive
On the count of every beat.
And you clap like this . . .

(Clap on beats one, two, three, and four. Repeat eight times.)

15

A Man Named King

Objectives

♪ To learn a song and narrative about Martin Luther King Jr.

♪ To improve singing skills

Skills

♪ Singing

♪ Dramatization

♪ Creative Writing

Music

CD #1, Track 16: "A Man Named King"

ACTIVITY

1 In advance, copy the lyrics of the song "A Man Named King" on an overhead transparency.

2 Display the transparency, play the recording, and have children read along silently.

3 Have volunteers read part of the narration and song.

4 Have children make up movements to dramatize the lyrics of the song.

5 Play the song again while children perform the movements to the music.

EXTENSIONS

• Include this song in a larger unit of study on the civil rights movement.

• Have children write their own lyrics to this melody with different subjects (e.g., We all love to play outside. Alleluia; One day we will be in charge. Alleluia; In this class we work as one. Alleluia). Use the new lyrics to create a class songbook.

A Man Named King

Words and Music by Greg Scelsa
Copyright 1989, Little House Music (ASCAP)

Once there was a man named King. Alleluia.
They called him Martin Luther King. Alleluia.

King was wise and he was good. Alleluia.
He believed in brotherhood. Alleluia.

Now Martin's eyes were color blind. Alleluia.
For he loved people of every kind. Alleluia.

He had a dream for you and me. Alleluia.
He knew that all men must be free. Alleluia.

The freedom road is weary and long. Alleluia.
But Martin sang a freedom song. Alleluia.

Then one day Martin sang no more. Alleluia.
But he had changed the world forevermore. Alleluia.

We must keep the dream alive. Alleluia.
Freedom's song can never die. Alleluia.

If we join hands it will come true. Alleluia.
For freedom starts with me and you. Alleluia.

Spoken:
*I have a dream that one day this nation will rise
up and live out the true meaning of its creed:
We hold these truths to be self-evident, that all
men are created equal.*

Once there was a man named King. Alleluia.
They called him Martin Luther King. Alleluia.

16

The World Is a Rainbow

Objectives

♪ To improve singing skills

♪ To dramatize the lyrics of a song

Skills

♪ Singing

♪ Reading

♪ Expression

Music

CD #2, Track 1: "The World Is a Rainbow"

ACTIVITY

1 In advance, make copies of the lyrics to the song "The World Is a Rainbow." Give a copy to each child.

2 Read aloud the song line by line, and have children echo in response.

3 Help the class create movements that dramatize each line in the song. Have children practice the movements as you read aloud each line.

4 Have the class create steady beat movements for the instrumental interlude in the middle of the song.

5 Play "The World Is a Rainbow." Lead children in performing the movements they have created, without singing.

6 As children become adept at performing the movements with the music, have them sing along as well.

EXTENSION

Create a multicultural unit of study on the diverse peoples, customs, music, art, and foods found in your community, state, or nation.

The World Is a Rainbow

Words and Music by Greg Scelsa
Copyright 1978, Little House Music and
Gregorian Chance Music (ASCAP)

The world is a rainbow
That's filled with many colors . . .
Yellow, black, and white, and brown,
You see them all around.

The world is a rainbow
With many kinds of people.
It takes all kinds of people
To make the world go 'round.

Now, you be you and I'll be me.
That's the way we were meant to be.
But the world is a mixing cup . . .
Just look what happens when you stir it up.

The world is a rainbow
With many kinds of people,
And when we work together,
It's such a sight to see.
The world is beautiful
When we live in harmony.

La, la, la, la, la . . .

Now, you be you and I'll be me.
That's the way we were meant to be.
But the world is a mixing cup . . .
Just look what happens when you stir it up.

The world is a rainbow
With many kinds of people,
And when we work together,
It's such a sight to see.
The world is beautiful
When we live in harmony.

La, la, la, la, la . . .

Reading Rhythmic Notation #2

Objective

♪ To improve the skill of reading quarter notes and quarter rests

Skills

♪ Reading

♪ Counting

♪ Rhythm

♪ Concentration

Music

CD #2, Tracks 2 and 3: "Slomo Mojo" and "Fast Forward"

ACTIVITY

1 In advance, copy the following example on a chalkboard or chart paper. Be sure to make the notation large enough for the entire class to read.

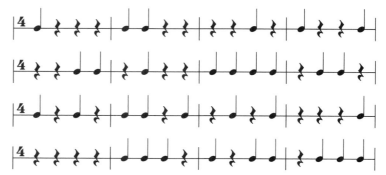

2 Review the names and functions of the notes and the rests as previously discussed in Lesson 13.

3 Have the class read (clapping and resting) the measures as they count "1, 2, 3, 4" for each measure. Go slowly the first time through the example, making sure everyone can keep up. As you repeat the exercise, gradually pick up the tempo.

4 Have volunteers perform the music in front of the class. Repeat as desired. As a reward, allow volunteers to perform the music on classroom percussion instruments.

EXTENSIONS

• Write a series of different beats and rests on a chalkboard or chart paper. Ask for volunteers to clap or rest according to the notation. Have the volunteers create new movements for the class to follow while they read (clapping and resting) the notations.

• Have the class clap and rest to the songs "Slomo Mojo" and "Fast Forward."

An Adventure in Space

Objective

♪ To act out the narration of a short story

ACTIVITY

1 Have the class stand in an area where they have room to move their bodies freely.

2 Tell children that they are about to hear a story called "An Adventure in Space."

3 Encourage children to use their imaginations to create their own individual movements to act out the story.

4 Play the recording, and have the class act out the narration. Repeat as desired.

Skills

♪ Listening

♪ Dramatic Expression

EXTENSIONS

• Have children use boxes, aluminum foil, paper bags, wrapping paper rolls, buttons, and glue to create space suits, oxygen tanks, and other space props. Play "An Adventure in Space," and allow children to act out the story using their props.

• Bring in freeze-dried astronaut food for children to taste.

Music

CD #2, Track 4: "An Adventure in Space"

An Adventure in Space

Words by Corky Green
Copyright 1983, '84, Little House Music (ASCAP)

Get ready to blast off for a trip into space. It's time to get into our space suits. Step in with one leg and now the other leg. Put in one arm and now the other arm. Good job!

Now that we're all suited up, let's step into the launch pad elevator and ride up to the spaceship.

The doors are open. Now, step inside our spacecraft. We make ready to blast off. Fasten your safety belts, and hold on tight.

All systems go. Minus ten and counting. Nine, eight, seven, six, five, four, three, two, one, LIFT OFF!

We're in outer space! And now we prepare to leave our spacecraft and take a walk in space. Put on your air tanks. Tighten your helmet. Make sure the lines are attached safely around your waist so you won't drift away.

O.K.! Let's open the door. Get ready to jump into space. One, two, three, JUMP!

Now that we're outside the spacecraft, we float freely about—slowly. It feels just like we're swimming, ever so lazily. Look out—a shower of meteors! Move about. Don't let them hit you! Keep dodging those meteors. Don't stop moving.

Phew! It's over. Everyone stop moving. We're safe. Now, let's pull our safety line so we can return to our space shuttle. Pull with one hand and now the other hand. One hand and the other hand. Keep pulling. Good!

Now, let's climb inside our spacecraft. We're inside and safe at last. Now, take off your air tanks and your helmet and fasten your safety belts.

This is Houston Control. This is Houston Control. Prepare for re-entry, prepare for re-entry. Now, let's prepare our space shuttle for re-entry. Get ready to start engines. When I count to three, push your starter button on the computer console: one, two, three.

Good job! And now home we go—home to earth. Get ready for re-entry. Everybody hold tight as we break the sound barrier.

Well done! You're a great crew. Now hold on to that steering wheel as we begin our glide into the airport. Look out the window. Here come some jets to escort us in.

Look! There's the airport. Hold on to that steering wheel and let's bring the space shuttle down nice and easy. We're almost home. TOUCHDOWN! Great landing! You're sure good pilots. And now we taxi to a stop.

Now, let's open the door to the spaceship. Wow! What a surprise! Listen to that crowd and look at those TV cameras. What a hero's welcome. Wave to the crowd.

We All Live Together

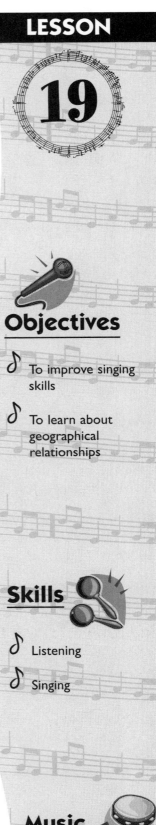

ACTIVITY

1 In advance, make copies of the six-page mini-book on page 63. Give a copy of the mini-book to each child.

2 Play the song "We All Live Together," and have children listen and follow along with the words at the bottom of each page of the mini-book.

3 Have children practice reading the words together.

4 Play "We All Live Together," and have children practice singing the song. Encourage everyone to smile while they sing. Repeat as desired.

EXTENSIONS

- Have children color and add details to their mini-book. Help them identify their state with a special color or mark. Then, have them cut apart the pages and assemble the mini-book, adding a cover if desired.

- Use pictures, maps, and a globe to reinforce the meaning of the geographic vocabulary used in "We All Live Together."

Objectives

♪ To improve singing skills

♪ To learn about geographical relationships

Skills

♪ Listening

♪ Singing

Music

CD #2, Track 5: "We All Live Together"

We All Live Together

Words and Music by Greg Scelsa
Copyright 1975, Little House Music and
Gregorian Chance Music (ASCAP)

Oh, we all live together,
Yes, we all live together.
Oh, we all live together,
Together every day.

We live in a house in a neighborhood.
The neighborhood is a part of the city.
The city's in a county and the county's in a state,
A part of the U.S.A.

And the U.S.A. is a good ol' place,
But it's still just a part of the place called Earth.
The good ol' Earth is out in space,
A part of the universe.

Oh, we all live together,
Yes, we all live together.
Oh, we all live together,
Together every day.

The Three Little Pigs Blues

ACTIVITY

1 In advance, collect several versions of the story *The Three Little Pigs*. Read them to your class prior to this lesson. Write the lyrics to the song "The Three Little Pigs Blues" on an overhead transparency.

2 Tell the class that they are about to hear a musical version of the story *The Three Little Pigs*. Display the transparency.

3 Play "The Three Little Pigs Blues." Track the text in time with the music. Encourage children to join in singing and reading.

EXTENSION

Ask children to compare one of the storybook versions of *The Three Little Pigs* to the song. Ask how the stories differ and how they are the same. Use children's responses to create a Venn diagram that shows the likenesses and differences.

Objectives

♪ To compare and contrast various forms of a story

♪ To sing "The Three Little Pigs Blues"

♪ To dramatize the lyrics of a song

Skills

♪ Singing

♪ Creativity

Music

CD #2, Track 6: "The Three Little Pigs Blues"

The Three Little Pigs Blues

Words and Music by Michael Lewis and Greg Scelsa Copyright
1995, Kiducation (ASCAP)

Spoken:
*Once upon a time there were three little pigs.
One day they were old enough to each
have a house of their own. But their mother
warned them to build their houses strong so
they would be safe from the Big Bad Wolf.
Now the first little pig was lazy, so when he
built his house, this is what happened . . .*

The first little pig
Built his house of straw.
He ran inside
When the wolf he saw.
"Little Pig, Little Pig,
Let me come in!"
"Not by the hair on my chinny chin chin!"
So he huffed and he puffed
And he huffed and he blew the house in.

Spoken:
*Well, the first little pig ran off as fast as he
could to hide from the Big Bad Wolf. Now the
second little pig didn't like to work either, so
when he built his house, what do you think
happened?*

The second little pig
Built his house of sticks.
The wolf came a-knockin'
Just for kicks.
"Little Pig, Little Pig,
Let me come in!"
"Not by the hair on my chinny chin chin!"
So he huffed and he puffed
And he huffed and he blew the house in.

Spoken:
*Well, the second little pig ran off into the for-
est as fast as his little feet would go. Now the
third little pig remembered what his mother
told him, so he built his house strong and safe.*

The third little pig
Built his house of brick.
The wolf came along
And he ran inside quick.
"Little Pig, Little Pig,
Let me come in!"
"Not by the hair on my chinny chin chin."
So he huffed and he puffed,
And he huffed and he puffed,
And he huffed and he puffed,
But he could not blow the house in.

Spoken:
*Well ol' Mister Wolf
He was awful bad.
He jumped on the housetop.
He was really mad.*

"Little Pig, Little Pig,
Down the chimney I go."
But the little pig had a boiling pot
Of water below.
OWOOO! Look at him go.
OWOOO! Well, look at him go.
Oh, yeah!

Show Me What You Feel

ACTIVITY

1 In advance, copy the lyrics of the song "Show Me What You Feel" on an overhead transparency.

2 Display the transparency, and lead the class in reading the lyrics in unison.

3 Play "Show Me What You Feel." Have the class silently read along.

4 Help children make up facial expressions and body movements to show the feeling named in each verse.

5 Have a different child read each of the 15 sections and lead the movements the class created for that verse. Have the rest of the class stand and follow each of the 15 movement leaders in time with the music.

EXTENSIONS

• Discuss the feelings named in "Show Me What You Feel." Ask children how they can appropriately express these feelings in a variety of situations—in class, between friends, with parents, and alone.

• Make a list of different feelings not mentioned in the song, and create movements to express them. Have children illustrate the feelings, and use their pictures for a bulletin board display.

Objectives

♪ To reinforce and expand understanding of the range of human feelings

♪ To learn to express a variety of emotions through movement

Skills

♪ Listening

♪ Reading

♪ Self-Expression

Music

CD #2, Track 7: "Show Me What You Feel"

Show Me What You Feel

Words and Music by Steve Sampler, Fred Koch, and Greg Scelsa
Copyright 1987, Treasury of Tunes (ASCAP)

Show me how you move when you're feelin' happy, show me.

Come on and show me how you move when you're feelin' shy, show me. Yeah.

Show me how you move when you're feelin' mad, show me.

Come on and show me how you move when you're feelin' tired, show me.

Show me how you move when you feel like dancin' around. Yeah.
Show me how you move when you feel like dancin' around. Yeah.

Show me how you move when you're feelin' sad, show me.

Now, show me how you move when you feel excited, show me. Yeah.

Show me how you move when you're feelin' strong, show me.

Come on and show me how you move when you feel afraid, show me. Yeah.

Show me how you move when you feel like dancin' around. Yeah.
Show me how you move when you feel like dancin' around. Yeah.

Show me how you move when you feel surprised, show me.

Come on and show me how you move when you're feelin' hungry, show me.

Now show me how you move when you're feelin' silly, show me.

Come on and show me how you move when somebody loves you, show me. Yeah.

Now, show me how you move when you feel like dancin' around. Yeah.
Show me how you move when you feel like dancin' around. Yeah.

4-Meter Composition

ACTIVITY

1 In advance, draw two one-line staffs (as shown below) on the chalkboard or chart paper.

4 | | | |

4 | | | |

2 Have each of eight volunteers create one measure (four beats) of rhythm.

3 Have children tell you whether they want a note or a rest on each of the four beats in their measure, and write their notation on the staff. Tell the volunteers that their measure must be different from their classmates'.

4 Have the class read (clap and rest) each measure while counting to four.

5 Select new volunteers to repeat the activity. (It is not necessary for the rhythms of one group of eight children to differ from those of another group.)

EXTENSION

Give each child a Writing Rhythms reproducible (page 64). Have children practice drawing and properly spacing a measure of notes and rests. Have children compose their own rhythms (four beats to each measure) on the four blank staffs. Ask children to make each measure different. Ask for volunteers to perform their compositions.

Objective

♪ To create rhythmic notation consisting of quarter notes and quarter rests

Skills

♪ Rhythm

♪ Creativity

♪ Permutation/ Sequencing

Music

There is no music for this lesson.

Everybody Has Music Inside

Objectives

♪ To improve singing

♪ To dramatize the lyrics of a song

Skills

♪ Reading

♪ Singing

Music

CD #2, Track 8: "Everybody Has Music Inside"

ACTIVITY

1 In advance, make copies of the lyrics to the song "Everybody Has Music Inside." Give a copy to each child.

2 Read aloud the song line by line, and have children echo in response.

3 Have children read along as they listen to "Everybody Has Music Inside."

4 Help children create movements that dramatize each line in the song. Have them practice the movements one at a time as you read each line. Also, help children create steady beat movements for the instrumental interlude in the middle of the song.

5 Play "Everybody Has Music Inside." Have children practice singing and moving with the song. Encourage everyone to smile while they sing.

EXTENSION

Have children write stories about things they like to do with music, the kinds of music they like, or why they like music. Ask them to illustrate their stories. Bind their work into a class book, and have them read their own story to the class.

Everybody Has Music Inside

Words and Music by Greg Scelsa and David Kirscher
Copyright 1980, Little House Music and
Gregorian Chance Music (ASCAP)

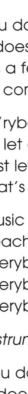

Everybody has music inside,
Especially for you.
Don't be afraid to let it out.
It isn't hard to do.

You don't have to be a virtuoso.
It doesn't matter if you sing just "so-so."
It's a feeling down inside your soul,
So come on, you can do it.

Ev'rybody has music inside,
So let a song ring out.
Just let it come right from your heart.
That's what it's all about.

Music is the sound of life
Reaching out for love.
Everybody has music,
Everybody has music,
Everybody has music inside.

Instrumental Interlude

You don't have to be a virtuoso.
It doesn't matter if you sing just "so-so."
It's a feeling down inside your soul,
So come on, you can do it.

Ev'rybody has music inside,
So let a song ring out.
Just let it come right from your heart.
That's what it's all about.

Music is the sound of life
Reaching out for love.
Everybody has music,
Everybody has music,
Everybody has music inside.

24

Old Brass Wagon

Objective

♪ To perform a traditional American circle dance

Skills

♪ Coordination

♪ Listening

♪ Cultural Awareness

♪ Singing

Music

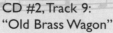

CD #2, Track 9: "Old Brass Wagon"

ACTIVITY

1 Arrange children in a circle, and have them hold hands. Tell them that they are about to learn an American folk dance and perform it with country music.

2 Have children practice circling to the left, taking four steps as they count aloud to four, and then resting in place for four counts. Have them continue circling and resting for four counts each until everyone can move their feet at the same tempo. Remind everyone to count aloud as they step.

3 Play the song "Old Brass Wagon," and lead the class in circling to the left in time with the music. Pause the CD at the end of the first verse. Lead children in performing the movements described in each verse before going on to the next verse.

4 Play the song again, and lead children in performing the appropriate movements in time with the music. Have the class sing while they dance.

EXTENSIONS

• Teach children different folk dances such as the German clapping dance, the Mexican hat dance, the Korean fan dance, the Israeli hora, and the Irish jig.

• Create units based on the history and culture of the people who created each dance the class learns.

Old Brass Wagon

Adapted by Greg Scelsa
Copyright 1980, Little House Music and
Gregorian Chance Music (ASCAP)

Circle to the left, the old brass wagon,
Circle to the left, the old brass wagon,
Circle to the left, the old brass wagon,
All together now.

Circle to the right, the old brass wagon,
Circle to the right, the old brass wagon,
Circle to the right, the old brass wagon,
All together now.

Everybody in, the old brass wagon,
Everybody in, the old brass wagon,
Everybody in, the old brass wagon,
All together now.

Everybody out, the old brass wagon,
Everybody out, the old brass wagon,
Everybody out, the old brass wagon,
All together now.

Turn around, the old brass wagon,
Turn around, the old brass wagon,
Turn around, the old brass wagon,
All together now.

Shoulders, knees, the old brass wagon,
Shoulders, knees, the old brass wagon,
Shoulders, knees, the old brass wagon,
All together now.

Clap three times, the old brass wagon,
Clap three times, the old brass wagon,
Clap three times, the old brass wagon,
All together now.

Toes and jump, the old brass wagon,
Toes and jump, the old brass wagon,
Toes and jump, the old brass wagon,
All together now.

Shout "Hurrah," the old brass wagon,
Shout "Hurrah," the old brass wagon,
Shout "Hurrah," the old brass wagon,
Give yourself a hand!

Objectives

♪ To learn the life cycle of a butterfly

♪ To improve singing skills

♪ To listen and follow directions within a song

♪ To dramatize the lyrics of a song

Skills

♪ Singing

♪ Creativity

♪ Sequencing

♪ Following Directions

Music

CD #2, Tracks 10 and 11: "Eensy Weensy Caterpillar #1" and "Eensy Weensy Caterpillar #2"

Eensy Weensy Caterpillar

ACTIVITY

1 In advance, display the words of the song "Eensy Weensy Caterpillar" on chart paper or an overhead transparency.

2 Discuss the life cycle of a butterfly with the class. List the sequence of steps in the cycle (as seen on the lyric page) for children to see.

3 Read aloud each line of "Eensy Weensy Caterpillar," and have children echo in response.

4 Play the song "Eensy Weensy Caterpillar #1," and track the print as the class reads along.

5 Help the class create movements to dramatize the lyrics. Have volunteers lead the class in performing the movements with "Eensy Weensy Caterpillar #2." Invite new leaders to repeat the activity.

EXTENSIONS

- Have children illustrate the lyrics. Use their drawings in a bulletin board display on the life cycle of a butterfly. Use this lesson as an addition to a unit on the life cycles of insects.

- Help the class create a class poem or song with the facts they learned. Use the melody from "Eensy Weensy Caterpillar."

Eensy Weensy Caterpillar

Words and Music by Steven Traugh
Copyright 1995, Kiducation (ASCAP)

An eensy weensy egg lies where it can't be seen,
In a leafy bush, lost in a sea of green.
An eensy weensy caterpillar hatches out one night,
And begins to eat and eat and eat every leaf in sight.

The eensy weensy caterpillar now has grown so big,
That it spins a chrysalis hanging from a sturdy twig.
Inside its chrysalis it will change as time goes by,
And when it does emerge, it will be a butterfly.

The butterfly, so beautiful, flutters 'round for days,
'Til she finds the perfect place for her eggs to lay.
Now an eensy weensy egg lies where it can't be seen,
In a leafy bush, lost in a sea of green.
Yeah!

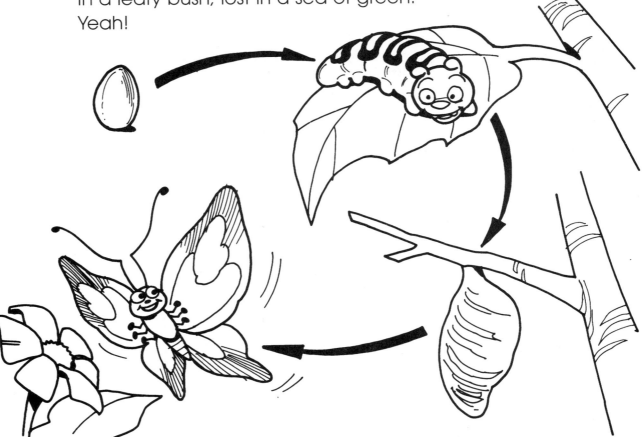

26

Down by the Bay

ON

Objectives

♪ To dramatize the lyrics of a song

♪ To improve singing skills

♪ To rewrite the lyrics of a song

Skills

♪ Singing

♪ Creative Writing

Music

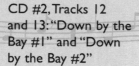

CD #2, Tracks 12 and 13: "Down by the Bay #1" and "Down by the Bay #2"

ACTIVITY

1 In advance, copy the lyrics of the song "Down by the Bay" on an overhead transparency, and display it.

2 Track the lyrics to the song as the class reads along. Read one section at a time, and help the class create movements that show the actions described.

3 Lead the class in performing the movements with "Down by the Bay #1."

4 Choose six children to lead the movements to each one of the six sections of the song. Have the six leaders form a line facing the rest of the class. Play "Down by the Bay #1." Have each leader step forward in turn and lead the chosen movement. Invite new leaders to repeat the activity.

EXTENSION

Help children create new lyrics to the song. Have the class illustrate the new verses, and use their work to create a class book or bulletin board display. Have children sing and dramatize the new verses with "Down by the Bay #2" (an instrumental version of the song).

Down by the Bay

Words and Music by David Metzger and Steven Traugh
Performed by Steven Traugh
Copyright 1988, Kiducation

Chorus:
Down by the bay where the watermelons grow,
Back to my home I dare not go,
For if I do my mother will say,

"Did you ever see a whale with a polka-dot tail?"
Down by the bay.

(Chorus)

"Did you ever see a goose kissing a moose?"
Down by the bay.

(Chorus)

"Did you ever see a bear combing his hair?"
Down by the bay.

(Chorus)

"Did you ever see a hog learning to jog?"
Down by the bay.

(Chorus)

"Did you ever see a snake eat a birthday cake?"
Down by the bay.

(Chorus)

"Did you ever see a fly making apple pie?"
Down by the bay.

27

Dancin' Machine

Objectives

♪ To imitate the motions of various machines

♪ To perform movements in time with music

Skills

♪ Creativity

♪ Rhythm

♪ Coordination

Music

CD #2, Track 14:
"Dancin' Machine"

ACTIVITY

1 Help the class create movements to imitate the following machines: washing machine, eggbeater, oil well, train, robot, and airplane.

2 Play the song "Dancin' Machine," and lead the class in steady beat movements. Stop the steady beat movements during the spoken instructions. At this point, lead the class in the machine movements as directed on the CD.

3 Stop the CD when the singing resumes. Ask the class to think of movements people make to operate various machines (e.g., typing, driving, vacuuming). List the movements on chart paper.

4 Play the rest of "Dancin' Machine," and have volunteers lead the class in the movements from the list

EXTENSIONS

• Have six volunteers each lead one of the six movements. Choose new leaders to repeat the activity.

• Have the class play a mime game. Ask one child to silently act out a machine, and challenge the rest of the class to identify the machine.

Dancin' Machine

Words and Music by Greg Scelsa
Copyright 1979, Little House Music and
Gregorian Chance Music (ASCAP)

Now everybody's body is a dancin' machine.
Come on and turn it on.
Get into the motion and see what I mean.
I said let's turn it on.
Get your body goin' like a motor movin'.
Everything is workin' and you can't stop groovin'.
It's such a crazy, crazy scene,
To see a dancin' machine.
Now everybody can be a dancin' machine.
I said everybody can be a dancin' machine.

Spoken:
Now twist like a wash'n machine.
C'mon now, twist. Yeah, like a washin' machine.
Okay now, do the eggbeater.
Spin your hands around together. That's it. The eggbeater. All right!
Okay now, spread your arms out and rock from side to side like an oil well.
Yeah, you got it, the oil well.
Now we're gonna do the locomotion like a railroad train, a-chuggin' down the tracks.
Well yeah, c'mon chug, chug, chug, here we go. Hey!
Okay now, be a robot. Do real jerky motions.
Hey, that's it! A robot!
Now everybody fly like an airplane.
Spread those wings. C'mon fly like an airplane!

We've Got the Whole World in Our Hands

Objectives

♪ To learn a song about ecology

♪ To improve singing skills

♪ To improve creative writing skills

Skills

♪ Reading

♪ Singing

♪ Creative Writing

Music

CD #2, Track 15: "We've Got the Whole World in Our Hands"

ACTIVITY

1 In advance, make copies of the lyrics to the song "We've Got the Whole World in Our Hands." Give a copy to each child.

2 Read aloud the song one line at a time, and have the class echo in response. Help children make up movements to dramatize the lyrics of the song.

3 Play "We've Got the Whole World in Our Hands."

4 Have several children lead the class in performing the movements as everyone practices singing. Invite new leaders to repeat the activity.

EXTENSIONS

• Include this song in a larger study of ecology.

• Have the class write their own lyrics to the melody on different topics (e.g., I've got my whole future in my hands, I've got a big hippo on my head, I've got twelve hamsters in my house).

We've Got the Whole World in Our Hands

Adapted by Greg Scelsa
Copyright 1991, Little House Music and
Gregorian Chance Music (ASCAP)

We've got the whole world in our hands,
We've got the whole wide world in our hands,
We've got the whole world in our hands,
We've got the whole world in our hands.

We've got the rivers and the oceans in our hands,
We've got the rivers and the oceans in our hands,
We've got the rivers and the oceans in our hands,
We've got the whole world in our hands.

We've got the trees and the flowers in our hands,
We've got the trees and the flowers in our hands,
We've got the trees and the flowers in our hands,
We've got the whole world in our hands.

We've got the air we breathe in our hands,
We've got the air we breathe in our hands,
We've got the air we breathe in our hands,
We've got the whole world in our hands.

We've got the whales and the dolphins in our hands,
We've got the whales and the dolphins in our hands,
We've got the whales and the dolphins in our hands,
We've got the whole world in our hands.

We've got the bottles and the cans in our hands,
We've got the bottles and the cans in our hands,
We've got the bottles and the cans in our hands,
We've got the whole world in our hands.

29

Ballin' the Jack

Objectives

♪ To improve gross motor skills

♪ To learn to line dance

Skills

♪ Listening

♪ Singing

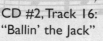

Music

CD #2, Track 16: "Ballin' the Jack"

ACTIVITY

1 In advance, copy the lyrics of the song "Ballin' the Jack" on an overhead transparency or chart paper.

2 Have children stand and face you. Tell them that they are about to learn a dance called "Ballin' the Jack."

3 Read the lyrics to the class one line at a time. Help children create the movements described. Have them practice the movements slowly in sequence.

4 Have a volunteer read the lyrics while you lead the class in the movements.

5 Play "Ballin' the Jack." Lead the class in performing the movements in time with the music. Repeat several times.

EXTENSION

Have children pair up and perform the movements with the music. Have one child in each pair lead and the second child follow. Replay the song, and have partners switch roles.

Ballin' the Jack

Words by Jim Burris
Copyright 1980, Jim Burris

First you put your two knees close up tight.
Then you swing 'em to the left,
And you swing 'em to the right.
You walk in a circle kinda nice and tight.
Then you twist around, twist around, with all of your might.
Shake your lovin' arms way out in space.
Then you bump, bump, bump with style and grace.
Put your right foot out and slide it back.
That's what we call ballin' the jack.

30

Friends

Objectives

♪ To improve singing skills

♪ To learn about feelings

Skills

♪ Reading

♪ Singing

♪ Creativity

♪ Movement

Music

CD #2, Track 17: "Friends"

ACTIVITY

1 In advance, make copies of the lyrics to the song "Friends." Give a copy to each child.

2 Read aloud the song, line by line, with expression in your voice. Have children echo in response. Encourage them to show their feelings while listening to the words. Help children create movements to dramatize each line in the song and steady beat movements for the instrumental interlude.

3 Have children practice the movements one at a time as you read aloud each line of the song.

4 Play "Friends," and have the class practice singing and moving with the music. Encourage everyone to smile at their classmates while they sing.

EXTENSION

Talk about what it means to be a good friend. Help children compile a list of the things friends can do for each other.

Friends

Words and Music by Greg Scelsa
Copyright 1983, '84, Little House Music and
Gregorian Chance Music (ASCAP)

Friends,
Everybody needs friends;
Someone to tell your troubles to,
To cheer you up when you're feelin'
blue.

Friends,
Would you like to be friends?
Would you like to share the day with me?
We can be anything we want to be.

Chorus:
 We all need each other;
 That's what friends are for.
 So, if you see someone without a smile,
 Give 'em one of yours.

Friends,
There's nothing better than friends.
I hope someday that I can say
That "Your friends are my friends, too."

Instrumental Interlude

(Chorus)

Friends,
There's nothin' better than friends.
I hope someday that I can say
That "Your friends are my friends,
And my friends are your friends,

Piggy Bank Spelling Game

One penny

is just a ___ ___ ___ ___ .

Five pennies

make a ___ ___ ___ ___ ___ .

Ten pennies

make a ___ ___ ___ ___ .

Twenty-five pennies

make a ___ ___ ___ ___ ___ ___ .

Fifty pennies

make a ___ ___ ___ ___ - ___ ___ ___ ___ ___ .

One hundred pennies

make a ___ ___ ___ ___ ___ .

One ___ ___ ___ ___ ___ ___

is what I'm saving

in my ___ ___ ___ ___ ___ ___ ___ ___ ___ .

Mini-Book

We live in a house in a neighborhood.

The neighborhood is a part of the city.

The city's in a county.

And the county's in a state,
a part of the U.S.A.

And the U.S.A. is a good ol' place, but it's
still just a part of a place called Earth.

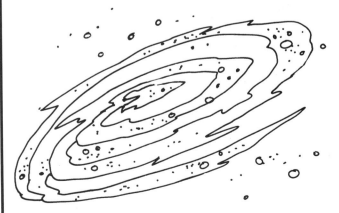

The good ol' Earth is out in space,
a part of the universe.

Writing Rhythms

1. Practice drawing quarter notes and quarter rests. Copy Example 1 and
   Example 2 on the blank measures beneath each example.

Example 1   Example 2

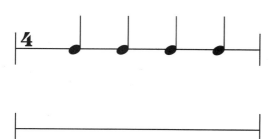   

2. Create your own rhythms in the blank measures below.
   a. Remember to make each measure different from the others.
   b. Space each note and rest evenly so they don't bunch together. (See Example 3.)

Example 3
good spacing   poor spacing